MEAN MACHINES

MONSTER TRUCKS

SARAH LEVETE

Raintree

www.raintreepublishers.co.uk
Visit our website to find out more information about **Raintree** books.

To order:
☎ Phone 44 (0) 1865 888113
🖹 Send a fax to 44 (0) 1865 314091
🖳 Visit the Raintree Bookshop at **www.raintreepublishers.co.uk** to browse our catalogue and order online.

First published in Great Britain by
Raintree, Halley Court,
Jordan Hill, Oxford OX2 8EJ,
part of Harcourt Education.
Raintree is a registered trademark of
Harcourt Education Ltd.

Editorial: Diyan Leake and Janine de Smet
Design: Michelle Lisseter and Keith Williams
Picture research: Rachel Tisdale
Production: Amanda Meaden

Originated by Repro Multi Warna
Printed and bound in Hong Kong, China
by South China Printing Company

ISBN 1 844 43174 6
09 08 07 06 05
10 9 8 7 6 5 4 3 2 1

British Library Cataloguing in Publication Data
Levete, Sarah
Monster Trucks – (Mean Machines)
1. Monster trucks – Juvenile literature
I. Title
629.2'24
A full catalogue record for this book is available from
the British Library.

Acknowledgements
AATAC: p. **51**; Bigge Crane and Rigging Company: pp. **50** (b), **54** (b); Bridgestone: pp. **5** (m), **12** (t); Corbis: pp. **5** (b) (Phillipa Lewis; Edifice), **17** (t) (Duomo), **19** (b) (Duomo), **29** (r) Minnesota Historical Society, **31** (b) (Bettmann), **35** (James L Amos), **36** (t) (Phillipa Lewis; Edifice), **43** (r), **50** (t) (John H Clark), **61** (Duomo); Ford: p. **16**; Dennis Taft (www.monsterphotos.com): title page, pp. **5** (t), **13** (t), **16–17**, **18**, **19** (t), **20** (t), **21** (t), **22** (b), **22** (t), **23**, **34** (b); Getty Images: pp. **4–5**, **14** (b), **15** (Tim Defrisco), **20–21** (Tim Defrisco), **25** (Bill Greenblatt), **34** (t), **46** (t) (AFP); G M Media Archive: p. **31** (t); Hawaiian Fire Department: p. **48**; Hulton Archive: p. **30**; Iveco (Tom Cunningham): pp. **37** (t), **44** (t), **44–45**, **45**, **60** (r); Kenworth: pp. **26–27**; Klaus-Peter Kessler: p. **24** (t); MAN-Nutzfahrzeuge: p. **57** (t); NASA: pp. **38**, **39**; Neill Bruce Photography: pp. **28–29**; Oshkosh Truck Corporation: pp. **47**, **49** (b); Peter Bull: pp. **8** (b), **13**, **28** (l); Peugeot: p. **56** (t); Scania: pp. **4** (b) (Dan Boman), **8** (Goran Wink), **11** (Dan Boman), **32** (Jonas Nordin), **33** (b) (Carl-Erik Andersson), **33** (t) (Ingemar Eriksson), **36–37** (Ingemar Eriksson), **41** (t) (Ingemar Eriksson), **43** (l) (Dan Boman), **49** (t) (Bryan Winstanley), **52** (t) (Jonas Nordin), **56** (b) (Johan Jonsson), **57** (b) (Goran Wink), **60** (l) (Goran Wink); Sparwood (www.sparwood.bc.ca): pp. **40–41**; STRANA: p. **27** (b); TRH Pictures: pp. **24** (b), **46** (b); Volvo: pp. **6** (t), **6–7**, **8** (t), **10**, **11** (t), **12** (b), **42**, **52** (b), **53**, **54** (t), **55**

Cover photograph of *Bigfoot* reproduced with permission of Action Plus (Neale Haynes)
The publishers would like to thank Mark Fisher for his assistance in the preparation of this book.

Every effort has been made to contact copyright holders of any material reproduced in this book. Any omissions will be rectified in subsequent printings if notice is given to the publishers.

CONTENTS

Any words appearing in the text in bold, **like this**, are explained in the Glossary. You can also look out for them in the Up To Speed box at the bottom of each page.

MONSTER MACHINES

Monster trucks rule the road. They carry the heaviest loads from tonnes of gravel to missiles, or even whole houses. Some monsters provide the most thrills at events as they rear up and crash into a waiting line of cars. Some are out on the road transporting race cars or moving tonnes of stone in a **quarry**. Other megamachines do the work that no other truck can cope with.

TRUCKS AT WORK

The working monster trucks that carry loads across the world are **heavy haulage** trucks. They are sometimes called **juggernauts** or **big rigs**.

It takes a long time to get a monster truck like *Samson* looking so good and packed with so much power.

big rig   nickname for large truck carrying heavy loads
heavy haulage   heavy loads

TREAT WITH CARE

Many monster trucks gleam in the sunlight. Drivers polish the chrome lights and the sparkling paintwork. Other working monster trucks have no time for such loving care. These huge machines are built for power, not for looks.

It is not easy to handle twenty gears and twenty wheels and steer a massive piece of machinery around a tight corner. It takes skill to drive one of these trucks. Before you even get to the controls, you have to climb up to reach the driver's seat.

FIND OUT LATER...

Which **pick-up truck** is the heaviest in the world?

What is the biggest tyre ever used on a truck?

What is a **toter**?

TRUCK BASICS

It is easier for an articulated truck to turn round tight corners.

There are two basic types of truck: rigid and **articulated**. Rigid trucks are built on a single metal backbone called the **chassis**, pronounced 'shass-ee'. Other parts of the truck such as the cab, engine, **axles** and bodywork are attached to the chassis. The chassis is made from strong steel so it can support the truck's weight.

BENDING ROUND

Most huge trucks are articulated. They consist of two parts. The tractor unit contains the powerful engine and the cab. The trailer is the load-carrying part that is towed by the tractor unit. Articulated trucks bend in the middle so that they can drive round tight corners. The tractor and trailer unit can be separated.

QUESTION

How can you steer a **juggernaut** with twenty wheels?

ANSWER

Have more pairs of wheels that turn in the direction of travel.

exhaust

cab

suspension parts

brake drum

front axle

axle   connecting rod between pairs of wheels that allows them to turn

A COMFY RIDE

Thundering down a bumpy mountain road could damage a delicate load. It could also be very uncomfortable for the driver. **Suspension** cushions the bumps in the road.

There are many types of suspension. In most large trucks, air springs are fitted at the rear of the truck. When the monster hits a bump, the air in the springs is squashed. The springs then bounce back into shape. They – and not the driver – take the force of the bump. Metal springs are used in the front part of the truck.

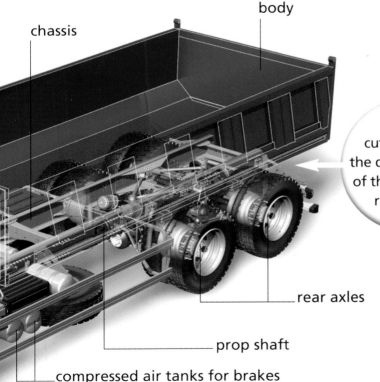

chassis

body

This cut-out shows the different parts of this Volvo FM9 rigid truck.

rear axles

prop shaft

compressed air tanks for brakes

suspension   system of air or metal springs that cushion the truck and driver from bumps in the road

POWER JUICE

Monster trucks usually run on a fuel called diesel, a special oil. Most diesel engines are **four-stroke** engines with four or more **cylinders**. A **piston** in each cylinder goes down and up, and down and up again. As the piston moves downwards the first time, it sucks in fuel and air.

As it moves upwards, the fuel and air mixture is **compressed**, or squashed, in a tiny space. This makes it hot enough to explode. The energy from this explosion pushes the piston down and powers the truck. The final up-stroke pushes out the burned fuel gases.

air pump

exhaust turbine

TURBO POWER

A turbocharger uses the exhaust gas flow from the engine to spin an air pump. This pushes more air into the cylinders. More fuel can be burned to increase the power.

The four-stroke cycle of an overhead valve, direct-injection diesel engine.

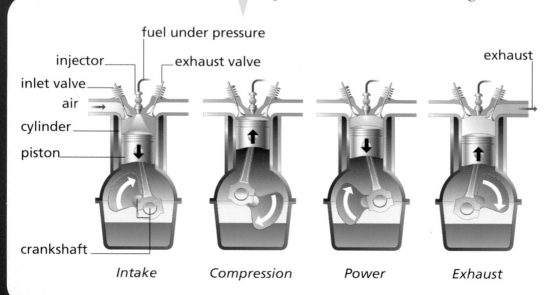

fuel under pressure

injector

exhaust valve

inlet valve

air

cylinder

piston

crankshaft

exhaust

Intake   *Compression*   *Power*   *Exhaust*

piston   rod that fits in a cylinder and is moved by the pressure of liquid or gas

DECODE THE DETAIL

'16-litre turbocharged V8 direct injection diesel develops 645 bhp and 2640 Nm at 1900 **rpm**.'

It helps to know what the technical stuff actually means:

- 16 litres – the cubic capacity or volume of the cylinders

- A turbocharger, or turbo, increases the engine's power

- V8 – the engine has two banks of four cylinders in a V shape

- Direct injection – the diesel fuel goes directly into the cylinder to allow increased compression of air and fuel, which gives more power

- Rpm means revolutions per minute – the speed at which the engine turns

- Bhp stands for **brake horse power** – the modern measure of the maximum power of an engine

- Nm – newton metres. The measure used for a truck's **torque**, or pulling power.

This is a brand-new power-packed V8 16-litre engine made by Scania.

DID YOU KNOW?
An 18th-century engineer called James Watt used the amount of work done by horses in a mining pit to measure a machine's 'horse power'. Nowadays, horse power often means brake horse power and is used to measure anything from mini-mopeds to mighty rigs.

torque   twisting action on the shaft that runs from the engine to the axle to the wheel

HAMMER DOWN

Megatrucks are designed to carry huge weights. It is amazing that they do more than crawl along when carrying the equivalent of six elephants. An adult male African elephant weighs about 6 tonnes and an average heavy load is 35.5 tonnes (39 tons).

BIG BROTHER

A trucker may be alone in the truck, but others are watching. In some European countries, a **tachograph** must be fitted to record the hours the driver works. Truckers must take breaks at set times to make sure they do not get too tired.

SHAPE IS ALL

Trucks with sharp corners and box shapes belong in museums. The smooth **aerodynamic** curves of modern trucks reduce **drag**. The engine does not waste energy battling against the wind.

For more about driving safely, see page 55.

aerodynamic   has a smooth shape that air can easily pass over
drag   effect of air on a moving vehicle that slows it down

STOP!

The weight of a load makes the rig zoom down a hill all too easily. Air brakes give the driver power to stop the truck quickly and safely. When the driver pushes the pedal, **compressed** air travels the length of the truck to the brake chambers at each wheel. The air pressure makes the brake shoes push against cast steel drums. The drums are attached to the wheels and **friction** stops the truck. Sometimes brake pads are squeezed against steel discs and these are called disc brakes.

SATELLITES CAN HELP

A global positioning satellite (GPS) system in the cab can work out the quickest route between two places. It can show the driver on a screen exactly where the truck is.

Wind passes easily over this truck's smooth, aerodynamic shape, allowing the driver to keep up speed.

---

friction slowing-down force of two surfaces rubbing against each other
tachograph device that records speed, distance and travel time

CARRYING THE LOAD

Fitting a huge tyre on a large truck can be a difficult and dangerous job. This is why tyres are often fitted within a safety cage.

In some factories, special machines fit and **inflate** the tyres for all the wheels that come off the production line. It takes just twenty seconds to fit and inflate a tyre.

RECORD BREAKER

The world's largest tyre is 396 cm (156 in.) tall, 147 cm (58 in.) wide and weighs 5.1 tonnes (5.6 tons). It was designed for 400-tonne (440-ton) dump trucks. The tyre can support a load of 100 tonnes (110 tons).

ALL AIRED UP

The air pressure inside the tyres takes all of the truck's weight. Higher air pressure can support heavier loads. Tyre pressure that is too low causes trucks to use more fuel than necessary. This can also cause **blow-outs**.

BLOW-OUT

When a tyre explodes, it can be very dangerous, especially at high speeds. The driver may struggle to keep control of the truck. Many rigs do not carry spare tyres because of the extra weight. The trucker must call out a mechanic to replace the tyre.

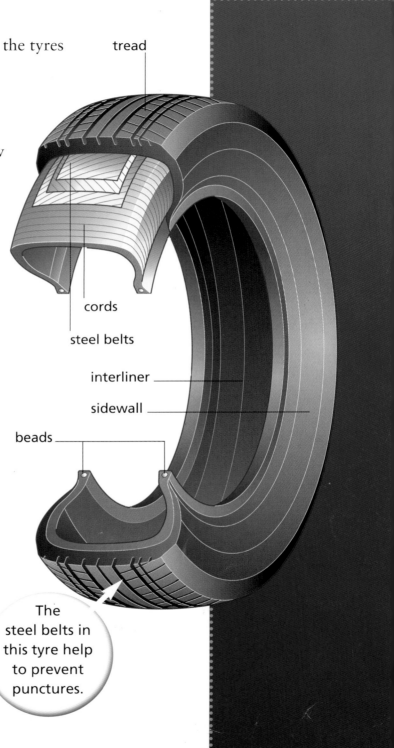

tread

cords

steel belts

interliner

sidewall

beads

The steel belts in this tyre help to prevent punctures.

MONSTER EVENTS

Competition and show trucks are special. To their owners, they are works of art and miracles of engineering.

UPENDED

With its powerful 2000 **brake horse power** engine, a monster truck can easily rear up on its back wheels and perform a **wheelie**.

MAKE-OVER MAGIC

These fantastic-looking machines are custom-built. Some are made from scratch. Others are based on regular **pick-up trucks**. The owner buys a standard factory truck – but it does not stay ordinary for long. A new engine, changes to the bodywork and a lick of paint work the magic. You then have a monster truck with great looks and amazing power.

logo   image or design representing a company

MEAN AND MAD

Unlike working trucks that travel long distances, these monsters are built for short bursts of speed. They break records and thrill crowds as they fly through the air. This is a sport for those who like their machines mean and massive.

LIGHT AND STRONG

In the early days monster trucks were made of metal, but now they are made of lighter **fibreglass**. This is painted with great designs and **sponsors' logos**. The **chassis** is a frame of lightweight strong steel tubes. The truck is covered by a steel structure called a roll cage. This protects the driver when the truck turns on its side or falls over backwards after lifting up its front wheels.

The custom-built, super-powerful engine is powered by methanol, an alcohol-based fuel. One monster truck can burn up to 9.5 litres ($2\frac{1}{2}$ gallons) of methanol per run. A run is about 77 metres (253 feet).

NO DOORS

Monster trucks have a hole in the floor. As there are no doors, the driver gets in through the hole in the floor! *Grave Digger*, pictured on page 22, is one of the few monsters to have doors.

Forget doors! Strap yourself in. This truck is for jumping.

DID YOU KNOW?

An average monster truck is 3.4 m (11 ft) tall and 3.6 m (12 ft) wide. To fit in with competition rules, it must not weigh less than 4082 kg ($4\frac{1}{2}$ tons). This is because a lighter truck can jump higher and move faster.

wheelie   riding the truck on its rear wheels with the front end lifted

HOW IT ALL BEGAN

A man called Bob Chandler wanted to promote his truck shop. He started to **customize** his Ford F-250 4 × 4 **pick-up truck**. He added huge tyres, extreme **suspension** and a more powerful engine. He named the truck *Bigfoot*.

Bob and *Bigfoot* started a new craze. The sport of monster trucks took off. In 1982, in Michigan, USA, Bob and *Bigfoot* entered an event organized by the US **Hot Rod** Association (USHRA).

RECORD BREAKER

Bigfoot holds several world records for the longest and highest outdoor monster truck jump and the longest monster truck **wheelie**.

It is hard to believe that the huge *Bigfoot 5* is built on this Ford F-250.

Weighing 12.7 tonnes, *Bigfoot 5* is the largest and heaviest pick-up truck in the world.

fleet   several trucks
hot rod   old vehicle stripped down and tuned for speed

Driving one of these monsters takes skill and courage.

THE BIG TIME

Bigfoot is now a big business. There is a **fleet** of eighteen monster trucks, touring and competing in shows around the world.

ORGANIZING THE SPORT

Today, there are many organizations **promoting** monster truck events, from shows to competitions and monster festivals. The organizations make sure the trucks fit certain safety standards. USHRA, the Monster Truck Racing Association (MTRA) and the European branch (MTRAE) all promote the sport.

SO YOU WANT TO JOIN IN THE FUN?

If you want to be a monster truck driver, you need to be at least 25 years old and have a commercial driving licence. Knowing about mechanics and metalwork is also important.

promote advertise

CRUSH!

More than 3000 vehicles are deliberately crushed each year. And people pay to see the destruction.

At a car crush event, old buses, vans and even aeroplanes are trashed as a monster truck slams into them. The bashed old vehicles come from scrap yards. They are returned there after the crush even more battered.

Before the event, any glass is taken out of the wrecks. This protects the crowds from shattering glass.

ADDING UP THE COSTS

It is expensive to run a monster truck team. The trucks have to be taken to events in special trucks. Monsters guzzle up expensive fuel. After a crush or jump, each truck may need some repairs.

Monster trucks cannot be driven on public roads, so they are transported in huge trucks.

throttle   part that controls the amount of fuel that goes to the engine

READY TO GO?

Helmet on. Wait for the green light. Check the safety straps. Put your foot down and go! Charge towards the parked cars. Full **throttle**. Feel the force as the truck lifts and then smashes down. Hear the crunch of the cars crumpling underneath the weight and force of the monster.

TYRES

At first, 1.2-metre (4-foot) diameter tractor tyres were fitted on monster trucks. But soon, drivers wanted bigger tyres. Today, monster truck tyres are over 1.7 metres ($5\frac{1}{2}$ feet) in diameter, and 1.1 metres ($3\frac{1}{2}$ feet) wide. These tyres are more often used on huge farm machinery.

THE RACE IS ON

The first monster truck events featured trucks rolling over or smashing up other cars. Soon, the crowd was calling for more extreme thrills. To meet the demand, the trucks started to race against each other.

NITEMARE

The latest *Nitemare* truck features:

- Dodge Ram **fibreglass** body
- 557 Keith Black Hemi engine
- Firestone 168 cm × 130 cm tyres
- Height 3.2 m
- Weight 4.3 tonnes

STYLES

Side-by-side racing involves two trucks racing alongside each other. In a freestyle race, drivers have a set time to show off their skills on the track. The fans are watching closely. They even get to choose the winning truck.

acceleration   ability to speed up
accelerator   foot pedal that controls the speed of the engine

TOUGH TALK

The word on the track is …

Burn out Spinning the truck's tyres to clear the mud off and gain **traction**.

Donut When a truck spins in circles in one spot.

Endo When a vehicle crashes and rolls end-over-end.

Gag it With the **accelerator** pushed right down. Also known as 'drop the hammer'.

Grab a footful Jumping on the accelerator. See also 'gag it'.

Hammer The **throttle**.

Hook up To get enough traction for fast **acceleration**.

Hot shoe A good driver.

Mash the motor Accelerate.

Sky wheelie When a truck 'stands' at a 90-degree angle with the front tyres in the air.

T-bone To crash head-on into the side of an obstacle.

STICKY GROUND

Tracks have to be laid and courses prepared for monster truck events. Some indoor tracks are made by covering the arena floor with fizzy drink syrup and a powder to dry it. This prevents the trucks from spinning wildly on the concrete floor.

traction   grip on the ground

Bigfoot is not too scary a name. But what about *Grave Digger*, *Nitemare*, *Sudden Impact* and *Maximum Destruction*? Truck names are meant to show the power and fierceness of both truck and driver.

LIFT AND BUMP

It is all very well to drive through the air. But what happens to truck and driver when they hit the ground? Monster trucks need monster **suspension** to cope with their gravity-defying stunts.

Grave Digger is up and flying.

axle   connecting rod between pairs of wheels that allows them to turn

SUPER SUSPENSION

After jumping 30 metres through the air, *Grave Digger* needs a cushioned landing. The **shock absorbers** take most of the impact. They smooth out the bounces. Also, they allow an extra 66 centimetres of movement in the suspension for the wheels to bounce up and down.

Safety is crucial at monster events as the unexpected can happen.

FOUR-LINK

Some monster trucks have a four-link suspension. This is made up of four bars linking the front and rear **axles** to the frame. Drivers can adjust the suspension depending on how much ride height they need.

SAFETY

To protect the driver and crowd, there are strict safety standards. Drivers wear helmets, gloves and fire-resistant suits. Each truck is fitted with strong seat belts and a fire extinguisher.

suspension   system of air or metal springs that cushion the truck and driver from bumps in the road

TOP TRUCKS

You may see the M561 1.1-tonne (1.2-ton) High Mobility Cargo Truck, known as the *Gamma Goat* (below), rocking and rolling on a truck trial. It is named after its inventor, Roger Gamaunt, and a goat, because it handles rough, rocky ground like a goat!

The British team driving the huge Tatra 813 in the Europa Truck Trials.

TO THE LIMIT

Truck trials are events that involve driving a large truck through a **quarry** or other very rough terrain. They are not for the weak-hearted. The aim is to finish the course. This is not easy when the ground is rugged and full of obstacles. Trials are often timed so drivers have to beat the clock.

EUROPA TRUCK TRIALS

In this European competition, the rules are complicated and the competition is fierce. You have to drive the truck between clearly marked gates without hitting them. The trial is not against the clock, so take your time!

customize   modify to a specific design
four-wheel drive   all four wheels turned directly by the engine

FOUR-WHEEL DRIVE

There are many events for 4 x 4 or **four-wheel drive (4WD)** trucks. These are 'off road' vehicles, such as Land Rovers and Jeeps, and trucks you are likely to see on the roads called Sports Utility Vehicles (SUVs).

Magnus Ver Magnusson pulls a 27-tonne (30-ton) truck more than 21 m (69 ft).

The engine on a 4WD turns all the wheels. On a two-wheel drive only the front or rear wheels turn. 4WD gives the truck extra grip in slippery conditions or when the truck is pushed to the limit.

TUFF TRUCKS

Tuff trucks are small trucks such as **pick-ups**. They are allowed on roads but their owners may have **customized** them with powerful engines and **suspension**.

HARD WORK!

Some people enjoy battling against trucks. In fun competitions, they test their strength in the strangest ways. They see if they can pull a truck.

---

quarry   deep pit used for digging up stone and sand

PROFESSIONAL RACING

Some trucks just race. They are made for speed. Drivers in supertruck racing are usually part of a large team of mechanics and designers organized by the maker of the truck. State-of-the-art engines, **suspension** and design give the truck a racing edge. There are separate truck races for people to enter their own trucks.

Inside each cab is a roll cage. This will protect the driver in case of a high-speed crash. Racing seats are fitted into each cab.

The Pikes Peak Hill Climb in Colorado, USA is a race that starts at an altitude of 2892 m (9488 ft). The 20-km (12.4-mi.) gravel course climbs to 4342 m (14,245 ft). There are 156 turns and sheer drops of 615 m (2018 ft) with no guard rails. Winning times are under 14 minutes.

This Kenworth T2000 takes part in the demanding 2003 Pikes Peak challenge.

lap   one complete round of the course
purpose-built   made for a specific purpose

COMPUTER TECH

Some cabs are fitted with the latest in hi-tech computer controls. **Sensors** fitted to different parts of the truck display information on a monitor about

- speed
- engine **rpm**
- **lap** time and lap number
- water temperature.

TECH TALK

Kenworth T2000 Pikes Peak Special
- twin turbo, 6-cylinder 18-litre engine
- 1375 bhp at 3077 m (10,095 ft) altitude
- 4.9 tonnes (5.4 tons)
- hand-cut tyres on rear drive wheels.

TUNED UP

The Super Truck Racing Association of North America (STRANA) races **purpose-built** racing trucks. Teams can use one of several approved engines. They make changes to give the truck its own style and power features.

This Tonka is purpose-built for the STRANA race.

sensor   electronic detector

27

TRUCKING DAYS

You need more than the steam from a kettle to power an engine. A coal-fired boiler keeps up a supply of boiling water. The steam from this pushes the **piston** out. A slide valve then changes the supply of steam over so that it pushes the piston back the other way. The piston is connected to a rod that turns the wheel.

Until the middle of the eighteenth century, horses pulled carts. These were the first vehicles to carry goods or passengers. In 1769, Nicholas Cugnot designed the first steam truck. This truck could travel at 5 kilometres (3 miles) per hour but only for 15 minutes. Solid wooden tyres made the ride very uncomfortable.

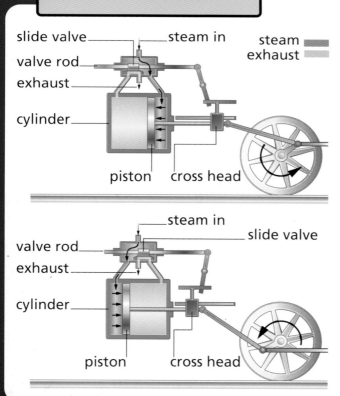

slide valve · steam in · valve rod · exhaust · cylinder · piston · cross head

steam
exhaust

valve rod · steam in · slide valve · exhaust · cylinder · piston · cross head

MORRIS'S SHREWSBURY

KF 6482

FULL STEAM AHEAD!

In 1892 Maurice LeBlanc produced a small steam-powered truck. It went at about 6.4 kilometres (4 miles) per hour – about the same speed as walking very quickly.

Soon the thick black smoke from steam engines was a thing of the past. Better engines that burned **petroleum** oils were invented.

In 1876, a German engineer called Nikolaus Otto developed an engine using a **four-stroke cycle**. He combined this with the use of more than one **cylinder** so it ran more smoothly.

OUTSIDE OR IN?

In a steam engine, the fuel (coal) is burnt outside the engine. In the engine designed by a French engineer, Etienne Lenoir, the fuel (petroleum oil) is burnt inside the engine. This is why it is called an internal **combustion** engine.

A 1931 Sentinel steam truck showing the steam boiler, chimney and steam exhaust.

MORRIS & COMPANY (SHREWSBURY)

This 1903 traction engine is driven over a block to show the power of steam.

‹‹‹‹‹‹‹‹‹‹‹
For more on the four-stroke engine, see page 8.

petroleum   oil found naturally in the Earth's crust

The driver had to turn a starting handle on this Leyland truck.

LEYLAND

In 1896, the first vehicle produced by the Lancashire Steam Motor Company in Leyland, England was a 1.1-tonne-capacity steam truck. Leyland Trucks now employ 1000 people and **manufacture** 14,000 trucks a year.

GETTING BETTER

In the early twentieth century, the Lacre Motor Car Company began production of motor cars and vans. These vans had simple **suspension** and electric lights. **Pneumatic** tyres replaced the hard solid tyres. An enclosed cab kept the driver dry and more comfortable. Truck travel was improving!

NEW DEVELOPMENTS

1915 The first separate tractor and trailer units were designed by an American blacksmith called August Fruehauf.

1929 Chevrolet's **overhead valve**, 6-cylinder engine with a volume of 194 cubic inches and 46 **brake horse power** was a first for the light-truck industry.

1950 The addition of turbochargers upped the power of trucks by a whopping 50 per cent.

1951 Chrysler's power steering directed the wheels on two front **axles** instead of one. This made it possible to steer heavier trucks.

1955 Chevrolet produced a V8 engine of 265 cubic inches and 132 brake horse power.

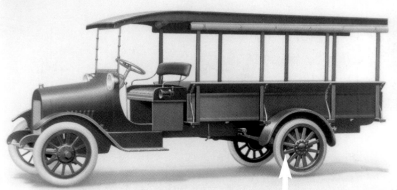

DIESEL POWER

In 1892, Rudolf Diesel invented the diesel engine for ships and trains. Later, this was used in trucks and heavy vehicles. It is a hard-wearing engine that uses up less fuel than a petrol engine.

Truck design has improved since the early days.

CHEVROLET

Chevrolet has been building and designing trucks for nearly 100 years. The first Chevrolet, or Chevy, was built in 1918.

WAR TRUCKING

During World War I (1914–18) trucks were used to transport troops and weapons across Europe and the USA. This was the first time that trucks had been used so widely.

In World War I, soldiers were taken up to the trenches in convoys of lorries.

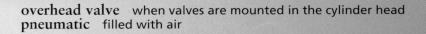

overhead valve   when valves are mounted in the cylinder head
pneumatic   filled with air

MANY MANUFACTURERS

Look around you at trucks on the roads. Some of these truck designers and manufacturers have been working for over 100 years.

Chrysler • DAF • Foden • Ford • Leyland • MAN Scania • Iveco

BUILDING A TRUCK

Massive trucks are built to last. With complex engines and specific details for each type of load, it takes months to design and build a truck.

A truck is first designed by engineers and designers on a computer. This is called computer-aided design (CAD). New truck designs are closely guarded secrets. Trucks that are better, bigger and faster than anyone else's can mean huge success for a company.

AN INTERNATIONAL APPROACH

Huge amounts of materials are used to make a truck, from **fibreglass**, aluminium and steel for the bodywork to shatterproof glass for the windscreen. Every part of the truck needs the best materials. These may come from all over the world.

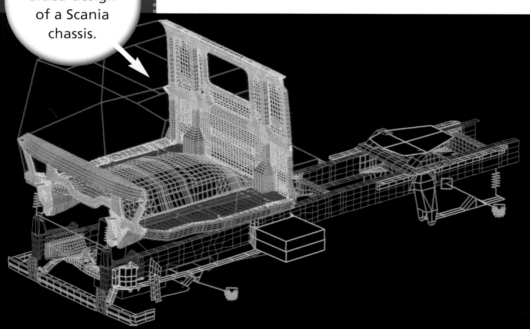

Computer-aided design of a Scania chassis.

prototype   first model used to test the success of the design

FIRST TRY

Before a truck is sold to customers, a **prototype** is made. The company can then examine its performance and safety, and make any changes. When they are satisfied, the truck can go into production.

A weight of 1.5 tonnes (1.6 tons) is dropped on to the cab to test its resistance to impact.

WHO'S WHO

Designers and engineers create new ideas for improved performance.

Mechanics assemble the truck parts from the **chassis** to the engine.

The production manager manages the team making the parts.

Safety inspectors check the truck meets strict safety measures.

The sales team advertise and sell the trucks.

TESTING, TESTING, TESTING

Trucks are crashed and crashed again. A team of experts tests the strength of the truck in case of an accident and work out how much protection the driver has. Instead of a driver, a dummy sits in the driver's seat.

A truck starts life as a computer design. After a long process, it is produced in a factory.

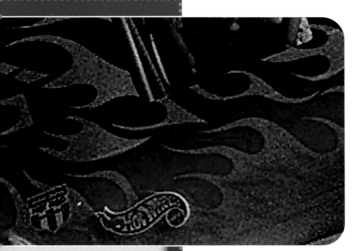

MAKING A MONSTER TRUCK

What is special about building a monster truck?

It can take from three months to one year to build from scratch.

It takes longer than **customizing** a factory-model truck.

LOOKING GOOD

The truck's power must be matched by dramatic looks. Faces, monsters, wings and flames are just some of the pictures seen on a monster truck. It takes more than a splash of paint to make these machines look so mean.

Some pieces, such as the **chassis**, are custom-made. A specialist company often makes the bodywork. The tyres are designed for another use but are adapted to monster needs. A team will put together all the parts before painting takes place.

This amazing suspension belongs to monster truck *Predator*.

WOULD YOU BELIEVE?

Because monster truck tyres are not made specially, it takes 50 hours to prepare a tyre. The tread of each tyre is cut by hand. This gives the truck more **traction** and removes weight by an incredible 204 kilograms (450 pounds) for each cut tyre. Before cutting, the tyre weighs approximately 400 kilograms (880 pounds).

LIGHT BUT HARD

If a truck is too heavy, it will not be able to jump or get up a good speed. But it needs to be strong enough to survive huge impacts from landings and crushes. Designers are constantly looking for improved materials to perfect the monster machine.

PAINT JOB

Special car paint is used for monster trucks. It is hard-wearing but gives off dangerous fumes. Painting the truck is done in a room with plenty of **ventilation**. The floor is kept wet to stop dust from the floor sticking to the wet paint.

MONSTERS AT WORK

We have seen monster trucks at play. But what about the trucks that do real work? These working trucks pull the heaviest loads, travel down the steepest roads or work in the most difficult-to-get-to places.

MOVING HOUSE

A **toter** is a house-carrying truck. The house is loaded on to the toter and driven to a new location. It is then unloaded and the occupants have the same house, just in a different area.

Only the meanest machines can get into forests, down **quarries** and even across rivers.

convoy   large group of trucks travelling together
           flatbed   truck with a flat cargo area

TRUCK POWER

Truckers know the power they have – and that is not just engine power. Trucks are powerful in other ways. A long line or **convoy** of trucks can block a road causing huge traffic jams. If truckers decide not to work, goods are not delivered, which means no fuel in the garage and no food in the shops.

BUILD A ROAD AND LOAD!

In the remote logging areas of Alaska, there are no roads for trucks to drive on. So roads have to be built first. Crushed rock and gravel make the road.

A truck called a loader scoops up bundles of logs in its huge bucket and puts them on to **flatbed** trucks. Each bundle can weigh more than 20 tonnes (22 tons).

TRUCK LOAD

Some trucks even carry other trucks. This Iveco transporter takes a Caterpillar excavator to and from the building site or quarry.

This flatbed truck can carry a load of 73 tonnes (80 tons).

toter   truck that can move a house

THE ROAD TO SPACE

People gasp and gaze in awe at space rockets blasting off. But do they know how the rockets reach their launch destination?

The Marion Crawler takes rockets and space shuttles to the Kennedy Space Centre launch pad. This is no ordinary truck. It makes any **juggernaut** look like a toy in comparison.

IN THE MAKING

The Marion Crawlers were designed by a team of engineers at the Kennedy Space Centre. The team decided to build the rocket Saturn V in a Vehicle Assembly Building (VAB) and then transport it fully assembled on one of the Marion Crawlers to the launch pad.

Each 2700-tonne (3000-ton) crawler can carry a 5400-tonne (6000-ton) Saturn V rocket several kilometres. The rocket has to be kept upright without leaning more than about 8 centimetres. The crawler is fitted with devices to keep the rocket stable. It is built for strength, not speed.

Since 1977 the Marion Crawlers have travelled an amazing 1986 kilometres (1234 miles). About twenty trips like this would take you round the world if you follow the equator.

The crawler's maximum speed is 1.6 kilometres (1 mile) per hour.

SLOW BUT SURE

The crawler rides on four double tracks, each pair the size of a bus. Inside its huge deck are diesel engines of nearly 8000 **brake horse power**. The engines drive generators that power electric motors for the tracks. The crawler burns 353 litres of diesel oil every 1000 metres (150 gallons per mile).

DUMP THE LOT!

Some of the most amazing megamachines are dumper trucks. They work in quarries and mines, and on large building projects.

A fully loaded giant dump truck can weigh an incredible 500 tonnes and have a 2700-**brake horse power** engine. Its tank can hold 4548 litres of fuel. Each tyre costs about US$25,000!

Imagine a bucket as big as a building. Now take a look at this picture of the Terex Titan, manufactured by General Motors of Canada. This is still one of the world's largest dump trucks. It can hold a huge 317-tonne load in its **hopper**.

PUTTING IT TOGETHER

In 1978 the Titan was brought to work by train in pieces! It travelled about 1610 kilometres (1000 miles) from California to a mine in Sparwood, Canada. On arrival, Titan was put together.

CHECK IT OUT

Terex Titan Facts
- Weight: 236 tonnes (260 tons)
- Maximum load: 317 tonnes (349 tons)
- Tyre diameter: 338 cm (11 ft)
- Tyre weight: 3600 kg (4 tons)
- Fuel tank: holds 3028 litres (800 gal.) of fuel

hopper   huge bucket holding materials such as rock or grain

TITANIC

The Titan is powered by a 16-**cylinder**, 3300 brake horse power **locomotive** engine. The engine is used with a generator to deliver power to four **traction** motors located on the rear wheels. The generator is powerful enough to supply electricity to 250 modern homes.

TECH TALK

The back of a dumper is raised by a **hydraulic** ram. This is a **piston** that is forced along a tube by oil pressure. It is powered by the dumper's engine.

The Terex Titan is one of the largest trucks in the world.

---

hydraulic   moved or worked by liquid under pressure
locomotive   railway vehicle used for pulling trains

Truck: Kenworth
C501T truck

Length: 79 trailers
measuring a
total of 1018.2 m
(3341 ft)

Combined weight:
1072.3 tonnes
(1182 tons).

ON THE ROAD

In the Australian outback, there are no railways. Roads are narrow. The heat is intense. Extremely long trucks called road trains **haul** huge loads over long distances. They consist of a tractor unit and several trailers hooked together.

PULLING POWER

A standard road train is made up of three 13.5-metre (44-foot) trailers. The 450-**brake horse power** engine is pulling 40 metres (131 feet) of truck. A twin steering **axle** under the front of one trailer is hooked up to the back of the trailer in front of it with solid metal bars.

The typical load of a three-trailer road train is 120 tonnes (132 tons).

haul   pull
hazard   danger

DRY AND DUSTY

Conditions in the outback are harsh. Drivers often journey at night to keep cool. Searing heat and dusty roads test road trains to the limit. Special air filters protect the engine from the dry dust.

WATCH THE ROO!

One of the **hazards** of the road is kangaroos. They may hop in front of the speeding truck. A thick metal grill called a roo guard or bull bar protects the truck but there is little to protect the kangaroos from the truck. Let's hope they stay off the road.

REPAIRS

A **truckie** can drive for hundreds of kilometres before seeing another person. If the road train has a serious fault, a travelling mechanic may not be able to fix it. The road train will have to be towed to the next service station.

EARLY ROAD TRAINS

The first road trains in the 1940s used old US Army trucks. There were no brakes, so in order to stop the driver just took his foot off the **accelerator**!

This roo guard protects the speeding truck if it hits a kangaroo.

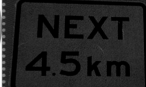

NEXT 4.5 km

>>>>>>>>>>
For more about life on the road, see pages 52–53.

truckie another name for a trucker

RACE ACTION

Motor racing circuits are busy with engineers, mechanics, drivers and state-of-the-art racing cars. The cars are not driven there on the roads, but are taken in a specially fitted-out truck called a race transporter.

A race transporter is not just a truck. It is a garage, a chill-out room and more!

WHEELS WITHIN WHEELS

The transporter has plenty of room inside for four cars. The upper **deck** holds this Ferrari F1 racing car and a race-ready spare car. On the lower deck are another racing car and a spare **chassis**.

HOME FROM HOME

As well as taking care of the cars, there is plenty of space in the truck for the team and drivers. A meeting room, work space and sitting area provide some home comforts. Here, the team can plan details of the race strategy. The truck is equipped with computers and satellite televisions. A fully fitted kitchen with a fridge full of tasty snacks makes it a pleasant journey for all.

The huge Iveco Stralis transports the Scuderia Ferrari Formula One team to the Grand Prix races.

SIDE-BY-SIDE

At the race circuit, these two transporters park next to each other. They have to be in position to the millimetre. Huge **hydraulic** rams then lift a second floor of office space, including two staircases, on to the trailers of the two vehicles.

The gruelling 11,200-kilometre (7000-mile) off-road trek called the Paris–Dakar rally takes vehicles through icy conditions, mountains and searingly hot deserts.

DESERT TRUCKS

Trucks need extra cooling systems in extreme heat. They have very large fuel tanks so they do not run out of petrol in the desert. The rough, bumpy ground bounces the truck around, so they need strong **suspension**.

AMPHIBIOUS TRUCKS

Some trucks are designed for both land and water. These are called **amphibious** trucks. Armies often use them to transport troops and weapons across small rivers. Some people use them as an unusual way to get around and have fun.

The Pandur drives through water.

amphibious   can be used on land and in water
hull   body of a boat

SNOW TRUCKS

Snow trucks are designed to stay stable in icy conditions. Extra wide wheels give them greater **traction**. Some trucks, such as the Oshkosh H series snow plough, can move over 1 tonne (2204 lb.) of snow per second.

GETTING WET

The Pandur is an amphibious six-wheel drive armoured vehicle. The engine powers both wheels on land and a **propeller** under water. It has an extended exhaust pipe and water jets on the back of the **hull**. It can 'swim' at a maximum speed of 11 kilometres (6.8 miles) per hour. In just 8 seconds the waterborne truck can turn around to face the opposite direction.

propeller   part with blades that turns to push a boat through water

PUT IT OUT

Water, foam, ladders, heavy tools, lifts – these are just a few pieces of equipment needed to deal with raging fires. To reach a fire, the truck needs to be fast and reliable. Combining a large, well-equipped truck with the speed and smoothness of a sports car is quite a feat.

EARLY FIRE ENGINES

The first fire engines were powered by steam and horses. A steam-driven water pump provided water to put out the flames. The 1901 fire engine, called *Firefly*, was pulled by horses. Before the fire fighters could get to the fire, they had to **harness** the horses to the wagon and light the fire in the boiler!

RECORD BREAKERS

This 1940 Ford, powered by two Rolls Royce 601 Viper engines, is a record breaker. This **customized** fire truck, called the *Hawaiian Eagle*, is still the fastest jet-propelled fire truck. In 1998 it reached an incredible 655 kilometres (407 miles) per hour.

harness   attach

DIFFERENT MACHINE, DIFFERENT USE

There are many types of fire trucks, used for different purposes. Many carry tanks of water on board and hold foam to deal with oil and chemical fires. Some fire trucks have a long arm called a boom. This can reach the highest places. Special legs called jacks keep the truck steady when the boom or ladder is extended.

DANGEROUS WORK

Exploding fuel is the main danger in this aircraft fire. The crews pump foam to put out the blaze. The foam blankets the burning fuel by keeping the air out. This stops the fuel burning.

The long boom sprays out water or foam, reaching close to the raging flames.

WEIRD LOADS

Trucks are often adapted to deal with very heavy and unusual loads.

A mining machine called a **dragline** was moved from a coal mine in Centralia, Washington State. A transporter was built which was made up of 24 **modules**. Each module is like a platform, about 2.5 metres (8 feet) wide. Each has four or five **axles** and each axle has four tyres. Six of the modules are equipped with a diesel engine, packed with 500 **brake horse power**. These power the **hydraulic** drive system.

AIRPORT TUG

Aeroplanes can fly. But they cannot drive along at slow speeds without starting the noisy engine. This rather small looking truck is powerful enough to pull aircraft short distances on the ground. The aircraft tug fits snugly under the aeroplane's nose.

This transporter has 432 wheels.

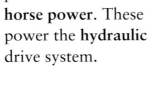

STEER

Imagine trying to steer 432 wheels with only 15 centimetres (6 inches) of clearance between your truck and a bridge. Instead of stressing out a driver, a computer took charge of the steering. It worked out the correct position of each wheel as the transporter moved.

The combined weight of the load and the transporter was an incredible 3810 tonnes (4200 tons). Tyres similar to those on a dumper truck supported this weight.

IT'S A WINNER!

Shaughnessy & Company, the company that succeeded in moving the enormous dragline, won the Specialized Carriers & Riggers Association 1998 'Haul of the Year' award.

RECOVERY TRUCK

To move a truck that has broken down, another massive machine is brought to work. With **hydraulic** lifting equipment, **winches** and steel cables, the recovery truck can lift the heaviest of trucks.

For more about tyres, see pages 12–13.

module standard part
winch rotating reel that winds up a cable

MONSTER TRUCKER

A trucker's life is hard. The driver needs to feel comfortable and relaxed, even after hours on the road. Some cabs have a built-in sleeping area and a mini-kitchen with a fridge and microwave. Some are fitted with televisions and computers. But these are only for use when not driving.

A computer watches what is going on in the engine. A screen in the cab shows the driver what is happening. If something is wrong, like the oil level is low or the temperature too high, the computer screen will flash a warning.

Even drivers need to take a break.

A truck driver needs comfort and space in the cab.

FRIENDLY TALK

CB radio is a trucker's friend. CB stands for citizens' band. Other drivers channel their radios to the CB wavelength. The truckers can then 'talk' to each other. They often give themselves nicknames such as Blue Bob or Rubber Duck!

You may need a phrase book to understand truckers on CB radio. These are just a few of the phrases they use:

Back quiet I have finished my transmission and you may proceed when ready.

Hammer down Driving fast.

Harvey Wallbanger Dangerous driver.

Readin' the mail Listening to the CB, not talking on it.

Roger Yes or OK.

Ten-twenty Location.

WHAT DOES IT TAKE TO BE A TRUCKER?

To gain a commercial driving licence, a **rookie** driver needs to go to driving school. Here, the learner drives in a **simulator**. Video clips show what to do and what not to do in difficult circumstances.

Special courses give a driver skill in handling **hazardous** loads. These may be chemicals or very long loads, such as triple trailers.

Written exams and driving skills tests ensure the driver is able to handle heavy vehicles.

It takes skill to drive a machine as mean and massive as this one.

MACK

OVERSIZE LOAD

rookie   inexperienced

Truck drivers may have to drive in very difficult conditions.

TRUE OR FALSE?

Keep your eyes looking straight in front at all times.

Answer: False
You need to keep your eyes looking around the road and in your mirrors.

SAFETY TIPS

- Inspect the truck, check the tyres, wipers and fluid levels
- Do not drive when tired, upset, or unwell
- Keep to the speed limit
- Drive with headlights on in rain, fog, snow, at dusk and dawn
- Slow down at night and in poor weather conditions
- Keep a good distance between you and the vehicle in front
- Never use a phone while driving
- Expect the unexpected.

TRUCK TALK

Truckers have their own language:
Dragon wagon Tow truck
Flip flop Trucker's return trip
Going horizontal Going to sleep
Shiny side Top of the trailer

simulator   device that copies the conditions of a situation

TRUCKS OF THE FUTURE

H²O

This Peugeot H²O is a concept vehicle that is driven by hydrogen. It is an environmentally friendly fire engine.

Designers and engineers continue to work on improved designs to make trucks cleaner, quieter and safer. These ideas are often developed into a **prototype** or **concept** truck to see if the designs are working.

There are three areas that designers are working on:

- Cheaper, cleaner fuels
- Ways to make trucks lighter
- Experiments to reduce air resistance.

This future Scania tractor unit is first designed on paper.

concept truck   type of truck that features the newest design

ELECTRIC TRUCK

One way to create trucks that are more **environmentally friendly** is to use electricity as well as ordinary fuel.

A prototype electric truck has been produced that runs on either diesel or electricity. The **hybrid** electric vehicle drastically cuts down on the pollution created by diesel engines. The truck is quiet, smooth and fast.

This designer is working on a clay model of a future MAN cab.

FUEL CELLS

The fuel cell is being developed. It uses hydrogen combining with oxygen from the atmosphere to produce electricity very cleanly. Water is the only waste product.

In the future we are likely to see lighter, more **aerodynamic** trucks that burn hydrogen. They will have a smoother shape more like the body of an aeroplane.

MATERIAL WORLD

Materials like aluminium and reinforced plastics will make this Scania concept truck lighter. This will cut down on the amount of fuel the truck uses.

MONSTER TRUCK FACTS

EUROPEAN SUPER TRUCK RACING CHAMPIONS

Year	Driver	Truck	Country
2003	Gerd Körber	Buggyra MK002	Germany
2002	Gerd Körber	Buggyra MK002	Germany
2001	Stan Matejovsky	Tatra	Czech Republic
2000	Harri Luostarinen	Caterpillar-TRD	Finland
1999	Fritz Kreutzpointner	MAN	Germany
1998	Ludovic Faure	Mercedes-Benz	France
1997	Harri Luostarinen	Caterpillar-TRD	Finland

AUSTRALIAN SUPER TRUCK RACING CHAMPIONS

Year	Driver	Truck	Country
2002	Inky Tulloch	Volvo Aero	New Zealand
2001	Inky Tulloch	CAT Freightliner	New Zealand
2000	Inky Tulloch	CAT Freightliner	New Zealand

NEW ZEALAND SUPER TRUCK RACING CHAMPIONS

Year	Driver	Truck	Country
2004	Andrew Porter	Kenworth	New Zealand
2003	Inky Tulloch	CAT Freightliner	New Zealand
2002	Inky Tulloch	CAT Freightliner	New Zealand
2001	Robin Porter	Kenworth	New Zealand
2000	Robin Porter	Kenworth	New Zealand

Dorian Lugo has been a truck driver for 15 years. She has driven 1,630,542 kilometres (1 million miles) without an accident.

WORLD'S FASTEST SUPER RACE TRUCK DRIVER

Year	Driver	Truck	Speed	Country
2004	David Vrsecky	Buggyra	281.723 km/h 174.94 mph	Czech Republic

WORLD'S FASTEST PRODUCTION PICK-UP TRUCK

Year	Driver	Truck	Speed	Country
2004	Brendan Gaughan	Dodge Ram SRT-10	248.783 km/h 154.587 mph	USA

WORLD'S HIGHEST MONSTER TRUCK JUMP OVER A 727 JET AIRLINER

Year	Driver	Truck	Height	Distance
1999	Dan Runte	Bigfoot 14	7.24 m	62 m

WORLD'S FASTEST MONSTER TRUCK IN COMPETITION

Year	Driver	Truck	Speed	Distance
1996	Fred Shafer	Bear Foot	4.59 sec	91.5 m

Molly Morter won 'Rookie of the Year' in the 2002 Pikes Peak Hill Climb.

A 3.2-kilometre (2-mile) convoy of 14 trucks and 21 ambulances carried 500 tonnes (551 tons) of aid from Clonmel, Ireland to the nuclear-affected region of Chernobyl in 2002. The convoy travelled 4830 kilometres (3000 miles) through 10 European countries.

FIND OUT FOR YOURSELF

ORGANIZATIONS

DAF
www.daftrucks.com

Iveco
www.iveco.com

Kenworth
www.kenworth.com

Monster Truck Racing Association Europe (MTRAE)
www.mtrae.co.uk

Scania
www.scania.com

Super Truck Racing Association of North America (STRANA)
www.stranaracing.com

United States Hot Rod Association (USHRA)
www.ushra.com

Volvo
www.volvo.com

BOOKS

Gibbs, Lynne, *Mega Book of Trucks* (Chrysalis Education, 2003)

Graham, Ian, *Fast Forward: Super Trucks* (Hodder Wayland, 2001)

Jefferis, David, *Monster Machines: Trucks* (Belitha Press, 2002)

Johnstone, Mike, *The Need for Speed: Monster Trucks* (Franklin Watts, 2002)

WORLD WIDE WEB

If you want to find out more about monster trucks you can search the Internet using keywords like these:

- monster truck
- *Bigfoot*
- four-link **suspension** trucks
- road train
- supertruck racing
- truck trial
- extreme trucks
- *Samson*

Make your own keywords using headings or words from this book. The search tips opposite will help you to find the most useful websites.

SEARCH TIPS

There are billions of pages on the Internet so it can be difficult to find exactly what you are looking for. If you just type in 'truck' on a search engine like Google, you will get a list of millions of web pages. These search skills will help you find useful websites more quickly.

- Use simple keywords, not whole sentences.
- Use two to six keywords in a search.
- Be precise – only use names of people, places or things.
- If you want to find words that go together, put quote marks around them, for example 'world speed record'.
- Use the advanced section of your search engine.
- Use the + sign between keywords to find pages with all these words.

WHERE TO SEARCH

SEARCH ENGINE

Each search engine looks through millions of web pages and lists all sites that match the search words. The best matches are at the top of the list, on the first page. Try **bbc.co.uk/search**

SEARCH DIRECTORY

A search directory is like a library of websites. You can search by keyword or subject and browse through the different sites like you look through books on a library shelf. A good example is **yahooligans.com**

GLOSSARY

acceleration ability to speed up

accelerator foot pedal that controls the speed of the engine

aerodynamic has a smooth shape that air can easily pass over

amphibious can be used on land and in water

articulated bends in the middle

axle connecting rod between pairs of wheels that allows them to turn

big rig nickname for large truck carrying heavy loads

blow-out tyre exploding

brake horse power measurement of the maximum power of an engine

chassis strong metal framework on which a truck is built

combustion burning of fuel and air to produce energy

compressed squashed or squeezed

concept truck type of truck that features the newest design

convoy large group of trucks travelling together

customize modify to a specific design

cylinder piston chamber in an engine

deck floor or level

drag effect of air on a moving vehicle that slows it down

dragline massive mining machine

environmentally friendly does as little harm to the natural world as possible

fibreglass material made from glass fibres and plastic

flatbed truck with a flat cargo area

fleet several trucks

four-stroke cycle engine where each cycle requires four strokes of the piston

four-wheel drive (4 × 4, 4WD) all four wheels turned directly by the engine

friction slowing-down force of two surfaces rubbing against each other

harness attach

haul pull

hazard danger

heavy haulage heavy loads

hopper huge bucket holding materials such as rock or grain

hot rod old vehicle stripped down and tuned for speed

hull body of a boat

hybrid made of mixed parts

hydraulic moved or worked by liquid under pressure

inflate fill with air

juggernaut large truck carrying heavy loads

lap one complete round of the course

locomotive railway vehicle used for pulling trains

logo image or design representing a company

manufacture make or produce

module standard part

overhead valve when valves are mounted in the cylinder head

petroleum oil found naturally in the Earth's crust

pick-up truck open-bodied truck in which goods that are picked up can easily be placed

piston rod that fits in a cylinder and is moved by the pressure of liquid or gas

pneumatic filled with air

promote advertise

propeller part with blades that turns to push a boat through water

prototype first model used to test the success of the design

purpose-built made for a specific purpose

quarry deep pit used for digging up stone and sand

rookie inexperienced

rpm revolutions per minute – the speed at which an engine turns

sensor electronic detector

shock absorber device that reduces the effect of sudden bumps and shocks

simulator device that copies the conditions of a situation

sponsor company or organization that helps pay for an event or product

suspension system of air or metal springs that cushion the truck and driver from bumps in the road

tachograph device that records speed, distance and travel time

throttle part that controls the amount of fuel that goes to the engine

torque twisting action on the shaft that runs from the engine to the axle to the wheel

toter truck that can move a house

traction grip on the ground

truckie another name for a trucker

ventilation air flow

wheelie riding the truck on its rear wheels with the front end lifted

winch rotating reel that winds up a cable

INDEX

Titles in the *Mean Machines* series include:

Hardback   1 844 43164 9

Hardback   1 844 43161 4

Hardback   1 844 43172 X

Hardback   1 844 43174 6

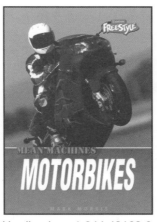

Hardback   1 844 43163 0

Hardback   1 844 43162 2

Hardback   1 844 43173 8

Hardback   1 844 43171 1

Find out about the other titles in this series on our website www.raintreepublishers.co.uk